emelia grant

the end of an evening cigarette

written by emelia grant

emelia grant

ISBN-13: 978-0578475219

to the moments where time seemed to look back
at me and smile at the memories we had made
together.
to the people who held my hand amongst the
storm clouds and kissed my cheek under the sun.
to the lessons i learned and the chances i took
along this beautiful journey,
but most importantly, to the words.

emelia grant

courage,
dear heart.

-c.s. lewis

to c.s. lewis:
pages 110 & 111
a few of my words, inspired by yours.

build me cathedrals
out of your words
paint me masterpieces
on blue lined paper
tuck them in envelopes
and send them
to my lonely heart
show me that you still
want this
that you still
want me.

i miss the days when
effort was something
that was mutual
in our relationship.

when i didn't need
to use my
flashlight to
find the bed
because you
you always left
the lamp on
before falling asleep.

they called her witch

> inhuman
> bruja
> *redhead*

they branded her dangerous
due to the crown of flames
she wore on her head.
they looked at her in fear
fear of her appearance
> capabilities
> nonconformity

fear of her fearlessness

but amongst all of that fear
was beauty.
there was magic in her fiery countenance
and so,
> in their ignorance,
> > they overlooked

the masterpiece that was at their fingertips.

with her auburn hair
flying gently behind her
swimming in the waves
of the sky
flying along currents
made of dreams
intertwining with the breath
of our beloved Mother Nature

she spread her wings
and took one fateful step
even though she was afraid of falling.

-that is how she learned to fly

in this world
where conflict
is such an immovable
part of our society
the ability to
discuss
debate
agree
disagree
but also
respect
each other's
values and ideas
is truly
a rare and invaluable
trait
that not many
people possess.

what we need more than anything

is peace.
these wars we fight
with society
with politics
with family
with *ourselves*
have poisoned
our minds
our values.

we are the medicine this world needs.
we are the ones who can fix it.
we are the peace.
we (are) *the people.*

just as we are from the earth,

> our bodies
> an extension of the very thing
> that gives us life

> our souls
> connected to the ground
> we *grow* on,

we return to the earth.

> -be kind to our home

to every person
walking the streets
of a country
state
city
town
school
who feels like
their culture
is being
ignored
suppressed
abused
victimized
forgotten
remember that
i am here
i am writing
i am living
i am *recognizing*
your strength
your patience
your determination
and when you need
to remember that
look for me
in these pages.

-your battle is my battle

the first thing i see when

i look at my mother
is a woman blessed with strength
patience
kindness
generosity
selflessness
a woman who wakes with the sun
&
sleeps with the moon
a woman who works just as faithfully at her job
as she does in her home
i see my eyes
the outline of a sister's face
the strong cheekbones of another's
the puzzle pieces of each of her daughters
i see the woman who catches my tears and
refuses to let them go to waste
combining that salt water
with her words of wisdom and advice
helping me grow
i see strong arms reaching out to hold me
i see solace
i see peace
i see what began as and will always be
my home.

her hair is thicker than any vein of gold
but still as smooth as the finest brand of whiskey.
her eyes radiate more light than any flame
but they appear soft in the evening's sunset.
her hands move more gracefully than any river
and have the capability to create
masterpieces
her body
silk
honey
soft
graceful
is stronger than you'll ever know.
but what *entrances* me the most
is her
strength
capability
intelligence
and
determination.

-those are the things that make her magic.

5.2.395
it's on these
fateful
snowy
days
the serenity

> surrounding those icy tufts of snow
> the millions of snowflakes
> coming to rest on thrones
> of evergreen branches
> the faded petals
> of a flower since past
> no longer woven in a simple crown
> coming to rest on golden hair
> reminiscent
> of fair Ophelia

nearly suffocates that small voice
in the bleak winter air
the small voice that is me
sitting on a wooden park bench
nestled beside a once magnificent river
now reduced to jagged ice
above smooth dark depths
and it is just outside the embrace
of Winter's cold arms
that i sit by this frosted windowpane
thinking
writing
dreaming
existing
the rest is silence

i live so peacefully
in this mind of mine.
my only wish
is that the peace
didn't dissipate
so quickly
when the
chaos of
everyday life
knocks
against my
eyelids.
most of me
accepts that
i must open them
and succumb to
another day
in this ritualistic society
but that peaceful part
of my mind
fights gently against the
never ending cycle.
it whispers softly
between the pause
of each knock.
stay here
it murmurs
i'll keep you safe
and my heart
breaks
as my eyelids
open.

her soul was art
but her mind was a prison
built brick by brick
by a cruel mistress
named Insecurity

the things you've survived
have painted a picture
so vividly across your
entire person.

you are a walking canvas
of hopes
failures
dreams
and deaths

people will stare,
trust me,
but it's only because
you're the painting
they'll never be able
to understand.

here i am
finding out for the first time
that the voices singing
most beautifully
are the ones
society tries hardest to suppress
maybe because
the words
they have to say
are not flattering
to the social standards
and ideas
set in place by the ones
afraid of music.

maybe if everyone
took a break
from the stupid
fucking
game of
let's see who can be better
we'd have a little
peace
a little
quiet
a little
kindness
and a little
happiness
in the world.

oh,
but these beautiful words
these breathtaking phrases
they haunt me so
they break my heart
they run their knives
as smooth as silk
over my open wounds
ensuring that
even if i heal
the scars will be there—
reminders growing old
with time itself.

-lemon juice

it's a funny thing
the emptiness
that haunts me
around every damn corner
it's the kind of solitude
that attaches itself
with absolutely
no
intention of letting go.
so i sit here
writing this poem
knowing that
this emptiness
is the one thing
i will never have to
say farewell to

-it would've been my easiest goodbye

how am i supposed to close my eyes
and greet my dreams in soft sleep
when my mind is so *alive* at this
beautiful hour of midnight

-rem cycle

when
the baby blue of your eyes
meet
the dark green of mine
i swear
it's as if
we're connected
in the way
that the tip of a paintbrush
connects to its masterpiece

daily reminder 1:

some people do not want to be saved

don't
waste
water
on
things
that
love
to
burn

pt.1

it's 11:43.
the power went out
about an hour ago
i'm under four layers
of blankets
trying to sleep
but
every time i close my eyes
i think of that
silly little silver ring
my parents gave me
when i was twelve.

pt. 2

do you remember that day?
we were sitting in the library
you were sleeping
on my shoulder
and
i was reading the book
you'd bought for me
the one with
those poems
the ones that always reminded me
of us
i kept slipping
that tiny silver band
on and off
my ring finger
until it finally
found a home on your
pinky
you were so
worried
it was going to slip off
that you would lose it.

pt.3

you even did
at one point
but soon after
you bought a
thick silver chain
so you could wear my
little ring
close to your heart
you told me
after you left
that the next time
we saw each other
you'd give that ring back
that it would be a
promise until then.

pt.4

you're
three thousand miles
away from me now.
we haven't talked in months
and
i saw a picture of you
the other day
you don't wear that
little ring
close to your heart anymore.
it's 11:52 now
but it's six hours
ahead of time
in Prague
maybe that's why
i can't sleep.

-midnight thoughts close to my heart

<u>muse</u>
and even though
you and i
were not meant to be
more than a Saturday spent
apple picking and
a couple of Friday nights
driving on dirt roads
i am still thankful
for the memories we made.
the memories
that are now
my muse.

i miss the flowers
and how they looked
in your hand
as you offered them
to me.
a small token,
a piece of your heart
that you picked
just for me

even though
you knew
in the end
those flowers
would shrivel up
and die
once we left
each other

-while it lasts

i'm tired
of loving
and not being
loved
in return.

-i'm giving that love to myself now

crimson leaves
falling from the now
ghostly
frame of that maple tree
we used to kiss under

worn footprints
from boots pulled on at dawn
when we walked hand in hand
along that familiar trail
to watch an autumn sunrise

warm hugs
offered at midnight
when i would wake up
from a nightmare
and find solace in your presence

the bitter bite
of winter tearing apart
everything we had built
in that beloved year

the cold goodbye you offered me
before walking away from us
to the arms of another

the ensuing nights
of tears and music and poetry

the growing that came from all of it

-things of autumn i am thankful for

i can tell you're thinking of *her*
by the way your eyes keep flickering over
to look at *him*
not in a possessive way
but more of an insecure way
i can feel your heart breaking
through those late night texts you send to me
when he's asleep
asking me what *she's* been posting on social
media
i can taste the defeat
seeping through your replies of
"don't hate him please"
&
"i know you're on my side"
i can see in the way that you walk
and talk
and smile
and hold his hand
that you believe what he did to you
what he did with *her*
was because you weren't good enough
or pretty enough
or smart enough
or skinny enough

however

i can't express these things to you
i've tried
but it was too early
too soon
it was before i even gave you the chance to heal
and, for that, i'm sorry
because you *need* to heal, my love
but
the medicine that will help your
heart
and mind
and soul
isn't something i can give you
it isn't something *he* can give you
it's something you need to give yourself
and i will spend each of my evening prayers
and midnight wishes
hoping you'll find that peace within yourself.

-i'll be here for you along that journey

society pushes
those quirky drawings
and unfinished paintings
aside
labeling them
as a child's daydream
or
an adult's unproductive hobby

but years later
when that child
has lost his innocence
and
that adult
has passed
the things
society considered
worthless
are looked at
under a new lens
and
become
art.

-we make museums for the things we used to
mock

the graveyard of imagination

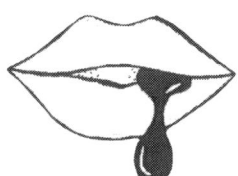

i'm sitting here in a classroom
crowded with these beautiful
individualistic
intelligent
valuable
human beings
that are being reduced to
dark circles
painted under eyes
now dull and devoid
of the childish light
that used to glow there

<u>daily reminder 2:</u>

if you didn't change for the better
than the change you made
wasn't worth the effort.

you shut me out
because my advice
was the hardest pill
to swallow.

everyone else
was feeding you honey
dripping from silver spoons,
but i poured you a single shot of
whiskey.

reality you couldn't handle.

i want to see
home
in your eyes
when they meet mine
before we kiss

i want to hear
adventure
amongst your footsteps
when you walk through the door
after a long day at work

i want to taste
wanderlust
on your lips
when they're kissing mine
at midnight

i want to feel
peace
as your hands
drift slowly down my sides
coming to rest on my hips

i want the smell of sandalwood and sage
to be my
my favorite hello
&
hardest goodbye
after your cologne has worn off
that old wool sweater
you gave me

i want *us*
to be
the journey of a lifetime
and
when we're done searching
the ends of the earth
i want *us*
to be our forever home.

-soul mates

she said,
"come with me. we'll travel the world."
he smiled softly,
"why limit ourselves to the world when the
universe is at our fingertips?"

the end of an evening cigarette

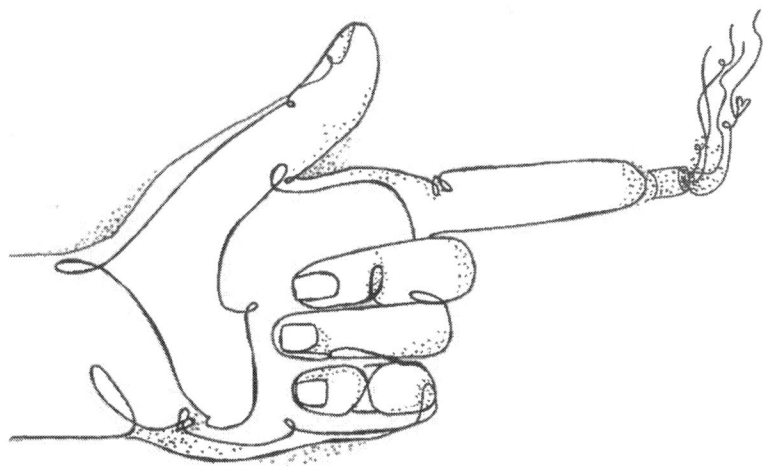

addressed to you

i hope you
are reading this

and know
that these poems-

the bittersweet,
they're about you.

i know we didn't last
and i'm sure i don't resonate
in your mind anymore
but
that playlist you made me

the one with those songs you played
as we walked under that umbrella
in the rain
to that little bookstore
to the art museum
to that quaint cafe
to that hole-in-the-wall pizza shop

still inflicts physical pain
on my heart
every time
kind woman by buffalo springfield
drifts to my ears
as i fall asleep at night

for one second
i truly believed that
i had lost my words,
but Independence
reared her beautiful,
terrifying head
and reminded me
that you are not
the only reason
i write.

<u>i feel loneliest at 3:00 p.m.</u>

the time in between,
when Sun
has long since reached her peak
and Moon
is still just a mere shadow,
that is the time of day
i feel empty
i feel somber
that is the time of day
that i write.

dream catcher

for years
i planted and watered
my dreams
until they finally took
strong and hopeful roots
and it wasn't until then
that i realized
the soil we plant ourselves in
is just as important as
the seeds we sow.

i must remind myself
continually
that
every word
every touch
every thought
must radiate
kindness
gentleness
positivity
because if i am not
a good example for myself
then i won't be a good example
for the people around me
who need something good
amongst all of the negativity in their lives.

<u>daily reminder 3:</u>

you are worthy of so much more
than you will ever know.

never settle for less
than what you deserve.

dear Doubt,

don't you dare try to convince me that
i'm not good enough
or
smart enough
or
pretty enough
or
talented enough

don't you dare try to convince me
that the ink spilling from my pen
isn't *artwork* in its most acute form

don't you dare try to convince me
that the music i create with my hands
and voice
is not worthy of being played
and praised

don't you dare come knocking on my door
trying to force yourself upon me
because i've seen myself for *everything*
that i am
and you cannot make me feel ashamed of that.

with a touch as light as smoke drifting off
the end of an evening cigarette
you tucked a strand of auburn hair
behind my ear
&
under the autumn glow of the setting sun
you said one last goodbye
but the reluctance in your voice
echoed to my ears as
"i love you"

-how your goodbye replays in my mind

the last time
i stared at a painting
you snuck up behind me
and grabbed my waist.

as i remember that
moment,
i am certain
your touch
was a more
complex
form of art
than any painting
we looked at that day.

<u>daily reminder 4:</u>

don't go looking for love, honey
you won't find it until it's ready to find you.

<u>bad directions</u>

i went looking for love
in a box of scratched records
in the end of a midnight cigarette
in the bottom of a whiskey bottle
and
i think somewhere along the way
i took a wrong turn
because
the only thing i found
was more of what led me there.

every time i see that polaroid
i'm taken back to a summer walk
to the local playground
where you kissed me on the jungle gym
and hummed kind woman by buffalo springfield
as you pushed me on the swing set

-is it childish of me to still think of you?

you are like a black and white film

something of the past

i keep rewatching

even though the ending

makes me cry

every

time.

cerulean blue reminds me of you

white sand beaches
carved with footprints from a different time
mosaic floors colored aquamarine and teal
three days of sunshine
blonde highlights in auburn hair and angel kisses
on rosy cheeks
broken buttons trailing down that shirt you gave
me
sunburnt shoulders encased in clean linen
a charcoal black suitcase packed too soon
one kiss at sunset surrounded by the smell of
sage and sea salt
three days of solitude
sunshine through a stained glass window
smoke drifting off the end of sandalwood
incense
the ashes leaving one last tangible trace
of us

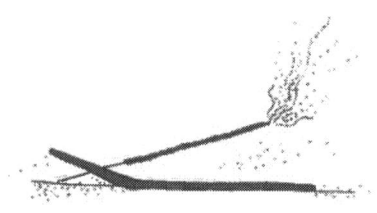

<u>unfinished</u>

i have been healing
for months now
but the thought of
what could have been
still haunts me
more than the
memory of what was

i keep thinking
that i've run out of inspiration
but then
i remember my mother
and her silent strength
i remember my sister
and her fierce tenacity
i remember my teacher
and her optimistic inspiration
i remember my co-writer
and her silent dedication

each time i'm reminded
that i will always be able
to find inspiration
in the
exceptional
talented
hardworking
empowering
women
i am surrounded by.

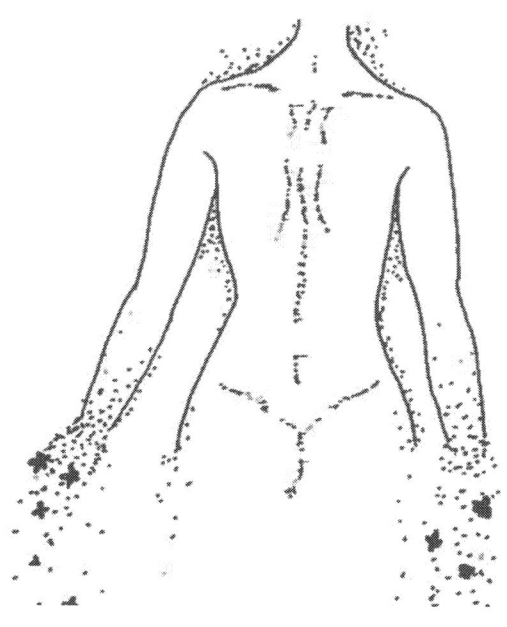

she is:

golden honey
and fairy dust
amongst polaroids
&
poetry

a blue and yellow flag
wrapped around her shoulders
proudly sharing her culture
&
language

a halo of incandescent sunshine
radiating throughout every word she speaks
a sprinkling of starlight in her eyes
&
laugh

a blush colored jacket
fuzzy like a koala bear
matched with Christmas wreath earrings
&
black boots

cup after cup of cafeteria coffee or tea
something about salty fries in a poem
chocolate and mint ice cream for heartbreak
&
hurting

a small gray table right next to mine
quick fingers typing poem after poem that i'll
someday read

a tiny red letter
sealed with a sticker
reminding me to choose happiness
&
self love

she is kindness
&
positivity

she is my co-writer

if this ever ends
you'll find me in that little perfume shop
where i bought you your favorite cologne

because
after i've burned
your valentine's day letters
that lakers hoodie
every polaroid
even the black book of poems you bought me

i know that there will be some part of me
still craving that part of you
and i know i'll find it
in a little blue bottle
filled with the scent of sandalwood and sage.

-my senses will betray me

i still search for you
every day,
perched on the window seat
by the door you slammed shut
the day you left.
it gives me a perfect view
of the horizon.

it's funny how the horizon looked
lonelier
when
your figure was walking away.

now,
as i walk towards the sun,
that loneliness is replaced
by *wanderlust*.

thank you for teaching me
that there is so much more
to this world
than an unhealthy relationship.

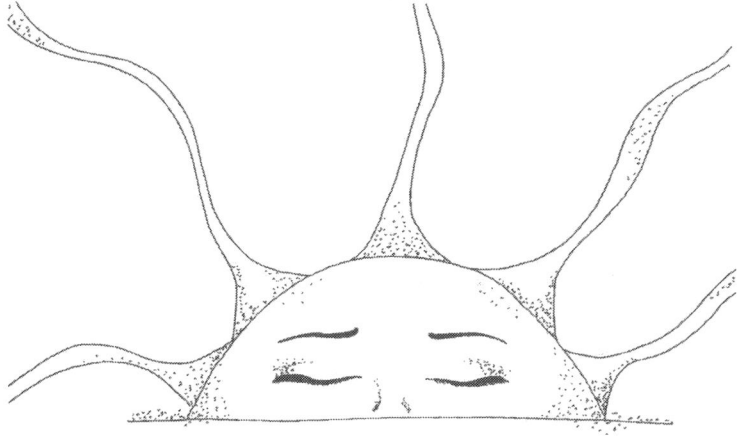

they scream at me
as my grades plummet like
their dreams of having an
Ivy League kid

it's not my fault

i whisper

the words never stop
it takes time to write
if i don't write i 'll burst

but they don't believe me

those aren't excuses

they say

manage your time
put your phone away

they don't understand

it's not that

i breathe

it's the words

-addiction

i've never been one to dream in color

instead,

      i dream
      in motion
      in shape
      in sound
      in smell
      in taste

it moves my mind
intoxicating my senses
with a wine so strong
the feeling
similar to a kaleidoscope
taking one emotion
and multiplying it
my senses
slipping into insanity
behind my eyelids.

it's like
god
laughed
when he
crossed my
path with
yours.

he thought
it ironic
to give
me
everything i
needed
and no
time to
appreciate it.

-time like liquid

if i had a dollar
for every poem
i read
or wrote
about you,
i'd have enough
money to buy
a plane ticket
to go see you.

-they say money can't buy happiness

i am from fireflies.
from fairies trapped in a jar.
i am from storybooks read by
my father's voice.
falling asleep on his shoulder,
lulled to sleep by the sounds
of a muffled television.

i am from summer evenings.
backyards doused in rain,
writing songs on an untuned guitar.
i am from late nights,
rereading favorite books,
tired eyes peering at the pages
from behind smudged glasses,
cadences of folk pulsing in the background.

i am from back roads.
driving faster and faster,
music blasted in the car
simply trying to escape.
i am from cool mist
hovering on a lake,
gentle waves splashing
onto the rocks,
greeting a hill of wildflowers
with a playful splash
and a quick goodbye.

i am from passion.
from aching fingers
pressing too hard on
worn violin strings.

from frustrated tears
at failed recitals.
i am from a breaking voice
standing alone in front
of my church,
looking for support in
the faces of god's children,
greeted by **silence** instead.

i am from slow walks.
sitting on bleachers,
sharing dreams,
holding hands,
learning a new language,
foreign words playing on my lips
almost as soft as the touch of his
i am from spontaneity.
from saying yes to the things
that scare me the most,
because i know in the end
the pain.
the fear.
the risks.
those are the things
i want to remember.

those are the things
i am from.

things that are loved by the sky

the sun
      the birds,
the flowers,
the trees,
buds yet to bloom,
fast cars,
dusty dirt roads,
a single vase of wildflowers,
perched on the kitchen table,
      the bees.
my skin, even the scars,
the angel kisses
freckled across my face.
the fireworks
raising their voices to
      say hello
while the sun closes
her eyes to sleep.
the quiet nights,
missed curfews,
carelessness,
that crinkled Polaroid,
captured memories
standing still,
and
i think
if the sky is anything
like me
it loves
      you.

someday i'll find you
on an island shore
a white sand beach
with sunshine in your hair
and the bay blue of your eyes
will hold a bittersweet hello
like the waves greeting the shore
before saying farewell
to explore with the tides

i do not love in halves
or quarters

i love completely
because that is the
one whole thing
i have
that has never been
broken.

-sliced peaches

i am so thankful
that the
shattered
pieces of my
heart
have healed
into the
mosaic
they were meant
to be.

-beauty is made of broken pieces

i poured myself into your hands,
your heart,
your mind,
your soul,
but never realized that you had no intention
of catching me.
my most vulnerable parts
were washed from your hands
slipping carelessly through the cracks,
dripping onto the pavement below.
forgotten as you walked away.

your greatest mistake
was loving me safely.

you had fire at your
fingertips

but you were afraid to
feel the warmth.

there is no alphabet in
existence
that will ever be able to
spell out
the words i need to say
to you.

-*i love you* will never be enough

my body
in the presence
of yours
begs for
your hands
to touch
mold
shape
sculpt
me.

under your
touch
i might as well
be clay
soft
supple
waiting patiently
for you to
push
and
pull
and make
a masterpiece
out of
our bodies.

he made love to my mind.

his hands commanded knowledge

out of me.

he challenged me.

and in that way

he loved me best.

how foolish we are
to assume that sex
is anything less than a
masterpiece

-intimacy is an art

"he's going to break you"

said the Brain to the Heart

"yes he is."

the Heart replied

"and I'm going to love every second of it

until he's gone."

every kiss you planted
on my cheek
continues to grow
long after you left
like a bouquet of
beautifully
haunting
flowers.

a wildflower
reminder
of what
could've been.

dear self,

i'm sorry for calling you ugly
when your beauty was right in front of my eyes
the entire time i was looking in the mirror.
i'm sorry i skipped breakfast
lunch
dinner
because i thought being smaller
would make me more desirable to the guy
sitting next to me in class.
i'm sorry i measured your worth
in Instagram likes and smiles of approval.
i'm sorry i forgot that you were perfect
without the makeup and hairspray.
i'm sorry i never gave you the chance to grow
without worrying what other people
would think of you.
you lost so much because of me,
because of my selfishness.
i should've told you this years ago,
but i was too worried about what
everyone else would say or think,

i'm proud of you, my friend.
i'm in love with you.
you've taught me that's it's okay
to love the insecure parts of me.
you've taught me to stop apologizing
to others
for loving myself.
i have better things to apologize for
and that begins with apologizing to you.

check all ~~that apply:~~

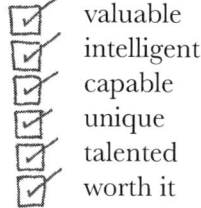 valuable
intelligent
capable
unique
talented
worth it

i constantly have to
remind myself
that every single
place and moment
is an adventure
of its own.

if i did not
repeat this
in my mind
every day,
the small town
that i was born in
the small school
i attend
the few new people
i meet—
they would suffocate
me.

i would drown
in the seemingly
insignificant lifestyle
i live.

but the mantra
"as soon as you graduate"
runs through my head
keeping me afloat.

it reminds me
that this seemingly
insignificant lifestyle
is paving the way
for the magnificent
days
moments
places
people
and
love
that i know
is coming
to me.

i unfolded my favorite wool blanket
and laid it across the damp park bench.

i uncapped my pen
and
opened my journal.

what i want from life
i wrote
is to love
to be loved
to discover
to be discovered
to seek
to find
but most importantly
to become.
i paused
to love myself
to discover myself
to seek myself
to find myself
to become *myself.*

-a letter to myself

the end of an evening cigarette

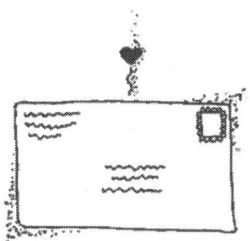

it's my smile
faced towards
the sun
that intrigues you.
you wonder
how it continues
to exist
even after
the pain you
knowingly
put me through.

but what you don't
know
is
underneath
that smile
are a hundred
more stories
written by people
just
like

you.

stained glass

i thank god every single day
for breaking me so completely.
he knew better than i did
that my heart needed to shatter
before i could solder the pieces back
together and form a masterpiece

if this ends
i know there will be pieces of
me
that will never heal

but in some ways
it comforts me
like a bed of soft ashes
greeting me as the fire dies out.

<u>the sculpture</u>

your touch
is fire
turning
the steel
of my body
to molten
metal

our hands
entwining
heat
the
the unspoken
words
between
us

they
weld
our bodies
together

forging
a
masterpiece

chasing sunsets

in the golden hour
as the sun sets
that's when you
think of
me
the most.

you
watch the sun,
burning into the horizon,
and face the reality:

i am every sunset
you wish you could capture

but never will.

seeing you
after all this time
i seem to have forgotten
(suppressed)
how it was
i used to hold you
when we were
(not)
in love.

-between the lines

eleanor rigby,
tell me
how your makeup
always looked so perfect
even though you kept
your face in that
little jar by the door?

-tell me the best way to fake it

never have i
ever
felt more alone
than i did
after losing
my most vivid
wish
when my eyes
opened
to reality.

-lucid dreams

it started to get better
and then i remembered
that you used to call me
princess.

-we can't be "just friends"

darling, i don't think my heart
would've broken so completely
if i had met you a few years later
than i did.

-young love hits the hardest

it's as if we are born
with this sickness,
this disease
insinuating
that we are not enough
without someone else
to complete us.

who taught us
that we weren't
good enough
to be our own
soulmate?

who taught us
that we had to
find someone to love
besides ourselves?

i refuse to believe
that there is no beauty
in *solitude*

-society feeds us lies by the spoonful

in reality
there will always be
another woman
another man
another vice
there will always be
something
that is trying to make you feel
like you're less than
enough
but remember
dear Heart
that there will only ever
be *one* of you
there will only ever
be one heartbeat
at a time
one breath
in a second
remember
that every seemingly
impossible
obstacle you hurdle
is making you stronger
for the things to come

-the things that will teach you to thrive

i think
we
as humans
just want
to feel
the love
we
are incapable
of giving
ourselves.

the end of an evening cigarette

i always liked the sound of
someday
as it slipped off your lips.

she knows your name
better than you do.
it's stained on her lips
from nights spent
whispering it
in the dark,
seeing how it
sounded entangled
with hers.

little did she
know
you
never
intended to
be in her
life
for longer
than the time
it took
for you
to break her.

silly girl
you fell in
love
with the
hangman
but you
can't even
see yourself
swinging.

-love is blinding

to c.s. lewis, whose magical words inspire me

this idea that magic
is only available in
the old books is a false
story sold to you by those only looking to clip
your wings. forget them. rely on the stories
of hope and imagination, the things of
an optimistic attitude that encourage
adventure and sponsor creativity.
that is where your wings will grow. it
happened to me, when i started to believe
in the impossible. in things like
Narnia and fairies
and pirate ships built from bedsheet sails. things
like Calormen, and evil dragons,
and sleeping princesses in tall towers.
the truths i learned from these outcast ideas took
me to lands i only ever dreamèd of traveling to,
here, there, and between.
to the places where i would eventually find the
deepest parts of myself in.
rising from the ashes of doubt i was raised in,
the idea of magic fed my deepest desires and
formed my golden wings.
like a phoenix from the age of knights
and kings
and queens,
i rose from the fire
when my critics least expected it.
i was my own religion. i made myself peter, the
first leader of my mind. it was empowering.

the fortress of my newfound independence was
built high up on my dreams and expectations. i
was both queen and king,
my confidence taught me lessons in pride and
humility. it taught me to share, to help others
find their Narnia and encourage them to never
give up,
even when the light of their magic is dim.
and, trust me, my dear, your old acquaintance
Doubt will come knocking,
his fist slamming repeatedly on the door of your
heart,
his brother Discouragement right behind him,
but it's worth the pain. just hold on tight
and trust yourself because Doubt and
Discouragement have an enemy: Hope.
his presence will dissipate the darkness from your
mind. it might take one, two, three...years for the
certainty to resonate in your heart.
take that time to encourage
sisters and brothers and any other human you
can find. we all need magic,
we're thirsting for it. let it fill your soul, drop by
drop. coronate it the
king of your imagination,
and i promise you, those women who crown
themselves queens
and mock your seemingly chimerical ideas,
they'll only ever rule
under you and under the magic Hope
encouraged you to pursue.
thank him.
he was the one who never gave up on you.

oh honey,
open your eyes.
Reality's a queen
and
you're
her next
bitch.

<u>to the people who discourage</u>

you are not living

you are simply
placating
yourself
so you can
make it through
another day
without going
insane
within
the confines
of your
limited
mindset

it was on a beach at 6 a.m.
cyprus grass bordering the sand
that you set your hand on my hip
and pulled me into a slow dance
the soft bronze glow of the sunrise
spilled onto your lips and set fire
to the words you spoke moments later

"with you, i would dance forever"

so with bare feet and sunshine playing tricks
with the ocean blue of your eyes
i spun around in a slow circle
and danced across the sand
to the music of your heart
making melodies with mine

i am most in love
with soft music.

the notes floating
through the air
intoxicate me
more than any other
wine
or
whiskey
i have tasted.

the feeling
of pen on paper
is honestly the most
intense mixture of pain
and pleasure.

my mind weaves
melancholy poems from my
memories
while my hand
paints softly on the
blue lined paper
of my favorite notebook.

it is both my sickness and my cure.

it is my addiction.

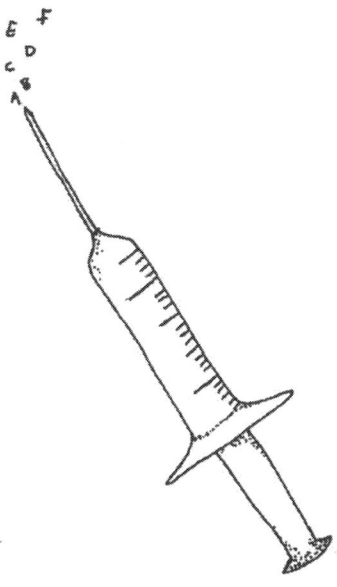

society brands abuse
as black eyes and screams at midnight.
what they forget to take into consideration

are the persuasive words whispered
constantly.
over and over again
until you're left with the hand of Obligation
held tightly around your mouth
as he murmurs quietly in your ear
weaving pretty little pictures through your head
quietly coaxing your fingers to start slipping
those
faded denim jeans off your hips.

they forget to mention those lovely strong fingers

the hands you love holding

how strong they are
wrapped around your wrists

shaking you when you
disagree or tease a little too much.

-abuse isn't always apparent

i knew it was time
to leave
when i felt more
black and blue
when you kissed me
than when you hit me.

evergreen said hello
with the most intoxicating
smile on his lips.

i wish now
that i had recognized
the taste of cheap liqueur
when i first kissed him
instead of mistaking it
for the rare whiskey he always
pretended to be.

-a wolf in sheep's clothing

the end of an evening cigarette

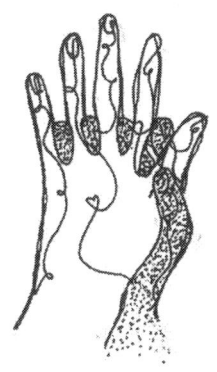

evergreen and me

evergreen laid beside me at midnight
his hand rested gently on my hip
a single honey strand of hair curled softly
against his caramel skin

if i wasn't afraid of waking him
i'd brush that curl aside with my fingertips

evergreen cooked me breakfast at six a.m.
bacon, eggs, toast, even a cup of that juice
i assumed he had forgotten that i loved
after washing the dishes he whispered
something about an apology
but before i could ask him about it
he fell asleep on the couch

if i wasn't afraid of waking him
i'd ask him if that apology had something
to do with the bruises on my wrists

continued

evergreen came home at midnight
he smelled like whiskey but kissed me
nonetheless
when i asked him to stop
he pushed me into the wall
next to a photograph
of our first anniversary
i held my breath as he shook me
i tried to focus on that honey colored curl
bouncing on his caramel skin
he only left a few bruises before releasing me
to go sleep off the whiskey

if i wasn't afraid of waking him
i'd tell him i was leaving for good.

evergreen always told me
that i was an open book
a library of thoughts
anyone could easily
see or steal
from me

how wrong he was

he never quite understood the
complexity
of my thoughts
he only recognized
what the confines of his small mind
allowed him to.

evergreen
only told me
he loved me
when he was
drunk.

evergreen only hit me
when he was
tired
drunk
angry
sad
happy
he never really saw the tears
that followed
as the bruises bloomed
like a wildflower graveyard

but one day
evergreen opened his eyes
at the sight of my tears
and all he said was

"i didn't think angels cried"

oh how i wished
i had possessed the wings of an angel
so i could've flown
far far away
from the hell
evergreen
forced me to live in.

too often
silence is the
loudest plea for help
the suffering
will be able
to utter.

-listen for the unspoken

carpe diem

what a perfect opportunity we have
to travel the world and cluelessly wander
with nothing but each other's hands to hold.

the end of an evening cigarette

for a moment,
i simply close my eyes and wonder
Love, what did i do in this life
to make you so generous?

-every moment is a blessing

with golden rays of liquid sun
casting themselves gently across her face,

i fell in love.

the simplicity of her smile upturned
to the sky was more intoxicating
than the whiskey
she had snuck into my coffee cup
the morning
after she had stayed the night for the first time.

loving you was like taking a deep breath.

it was a heady kind of feeling
but my lungs loved the taste.

-oxygen

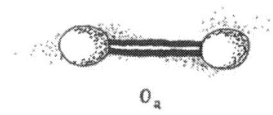

O_2

why are we so eager
to hit
fast forward
and waste time
wishing
our
childhoods away
but
when adulthood
comes
and
adolescence
leaves without
saying
goodbye
we spend
what's left
of our
young
years
working
and
complaining
and
wishing
we were
children
once more

-when will we learn to be happy
with what we have
in the moment

how refreshing it is
to know that you and i
have all the time in the world
to figure out our heart's desires.

-the little lies we feed ourselves

i think you and i,
in the most beautiful way,
are two timeless souls
living in a world
where we constantly feel
as if we're running out of time.

i truly believe in some
timeless
place

maybe one of Gatsby's
parties
or a 50's diner
a field of poppies
or that park bench
where
you said
"i love you"
for the first time

we will find each other
again.

-someday when the stars align

what happened to the careless, reckless, messy,
confessions we spilled to each other this summer

underneath that fading sunset
the same color of that wine we were drinking

everything seemed so simple
when we weren't worried about being
embarrassed

our only thought was to say as much as we could
before Reality strolled back through the door
with a hangover headache in tow.

-our courage doesn't have to be liquid

i texted a friend last night
just to check in
and
he didn't open the text
for a day

when he finally replied
i told myself
i had to wait before
writing him back

i didn't want to seem
too eager
or
desperate

i've been sucked
into that stupid
game
of who can
ignore who
the most.

-is this what conversation has come to?

can someone tell me why
the tired
bored
miserable
people of this world,
writers like me included,
continue to circle around and around
in this mistaken interpretation of life
instead of breaking the cycle
and living *for* something
not off something.

-we are born afraid to break the cycle

it's a struggle
every damn day.
and trust me, it takes courage
to break the one thing that never changed in
your life,
but you won't regret it.
life only comes full circle once,
and within that circle,
it's messy and hard and beautiful,
but outside that circle,
it's exquisite and unique and breathtaking,
so go test your boundaries
amongst the shattered pieces
of what tried to hold you back.

-we are born to live outside the cycle

i think they call it a crush
because
when the sentiment
is not reciprocated
you're left feeling
inconsolable and alone
with an ache for something
that will never happen.

i was too busy
fighting everyone else's battles
that i couldn't see
i was the one who needed saving.

-self care

look in the mirror and repeat after me:

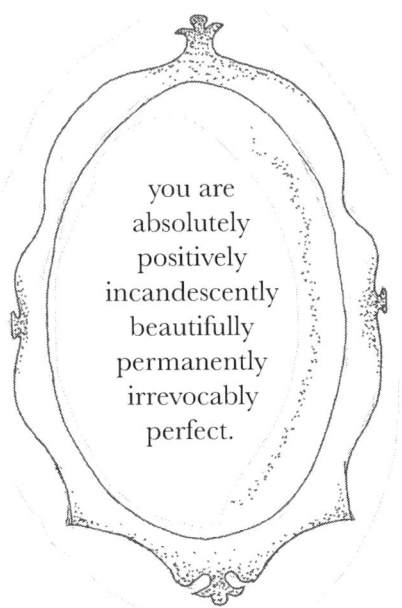

you are
absolutely
positively
incandescently
beautifully
permanently
irrevocably
perfect.

daily reminder 5:

stop trying to put yourself
first
in the life of someone who
continually puts you
last

i didn't think it was supposed
to be that easy.
to just smile and laugh and flirt
carelessly
simply
like kids.
i got so used to
complicated
with the wrong person that
normal
felt wrong with the right one.

the end of an evening cigarette

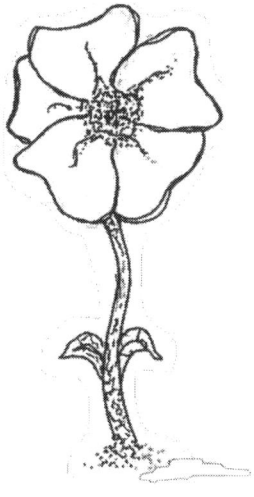

once i was loved
by this boy who
gave me
everything.
his touch
sent chills
of the warmest
softest
kind
down my back
and up my spine.
his kisses
made cold walks
in mid january
feel like july.
holding his hand
gave me a lifeline
when every
little
thing
was going
wrong.
he treated me
as if i was truly
his queen.

and in those
months
days
hours
minutes
that we were
together
i was loved
more fiercely
than any other
time
in my life.

-i hope my soulmate
is someone
like him

i am thankful
for my family
for my friends
for those
singing in the shower
moments
for laughter
for kindness
for a stranger's smile
across the counter
in that tiny cafe
for dusty roads
for
sunsets
&
sunrises
for music
for poetry
for feeling everything
in extremes
for tears at midnight

for first kisses
and goodbye hugs
for wildflowers
for autumn walks
for books
for reading
for simply
appreciating
my mind's abilities
for sadness
for happiness
&
for the opportunity
to think
to have
to write
to reach
the people reading
this poem.

<u>STOP</u>

take a   the stars
moment   are
and   beautiful
look up   tonight

the sun seemed to close her eyes
as we waltzed through those fields
dancing amongst the daisies.

and when the clouds blinked slowly
starting to cry
you grabbed my hand and
took off running towards
the twilight
that embraced the moon

your voice
bounced off the stars
as you laughed
and looked back at me

"we'll dance in the moonlight
if the sun refuses to be on our side."

to the ones spending Christmas alone

who don't put up a tree anymore
because the colored lights make
the end of a gun barrel seem more inviting
than the continuous Christmas music on the
radio

to the ones spending Valentine's Day alone
who used to send a dozen long stemmed roses
to the only person they ever truly loved
but could never seem to keep—
the one who lives a perfect life
sleeping next to the very man who put
a whiskey bottle
and
a nearly empty pack of cigarettes
next to the divorce papers
that True Love wanted filed

to the ones spending their birthday alone
waiting next to their telephone
warming their cold hands
next to that last flicker of hope
hope that one of their children—
maybe the one in New York
with two children of their own
or
the one in Seattle who swore
he'd make a trip for Thanksgiving—
would remember the 50th anniversary
of a forgotten human's birth

to the ones letting go because the rope
they were clutching so tightly
was untied by the one person
they thought they could trust
to the ones giving up Hope because Life
forced them to believe that they weren't worth
the blessed space they exist on
you are the ones worth remembering
you are the ones i will spend a lifetime
trying to memorialize in these pages.

-there will never be enough words to remember
the ones forgotten

pt.1

when i was 8
my teacher took
my pencil away.
she told me

"now is not the time to doodle."

she never asked
what i was drawing.

when i was 15
with pen
bleeding onto
my wrists
and
thighs
my mother took
my pen away.
she told me

"you'll get ink poisoning."

"you're ruining your skin."

she never asked
why i was drawing.

pt.2

after my pencil
was gone
and
my pen
no longer
offered me
an outlet
i turned to that
dear
sweet
razor
and carved designs
in my skin that
people wouldn't see
underneath
dark sleeves
and
darker jeans.

pt.3

when i was 17
my first boyfriend
said

"normal girls don't have scars like that."

he never asked
why they were there.

and so
on a perfectly sunny
day

while my teacher
was
solving
the Saturday crossword puzzle
with a pencil in hand
my mother was
signing her name
on a nearly empty
guest book
blinking fast
so any errant tears
wouldn't tarnish
those
lonely pages

pt.4

that foolish
young boy
was checking his
cellphone
sitting near the back
in a pew
where my mother
wouldn't
notice him

i was remembered
&
i was buried
with no
pencil no
pen and
years of scars.

-we take away the outlets our youth need

what happened to
the spontaneity
the risk
the adventure
the things in life that
make your heart hurt
from beating so hard

when did bravery
get replaced by comfort?

when did living
simply become existing?

the end of an evening cigarette

our voices
entwined,
like the vines
of that morning glory
growing beneath your window,
as we lifted
our eyes
to the sky
and screamed.

our insanity
echoed
off the mountainside
we had just climbed.

it felt
liberating
to simply express
our emotions
in a way
we hadn't
since childhood.

-wild things

<u>daily reminder 6:</u>

when you get the chance
to howl at the moon
and
scream to the sun
take it.

breaking

and even though
you *beg* for
atonement
i refuse
to give you
even an ounce
of satisfaction

i've learned
my lesson
from the
last time

when i gave
and gave
and you stole
miles
and miles
of me

you drained me
until there was
nothing
left
but
an empty shell
of who i was
before you
robbed me.

<u>building</u>

but now
you're back

you walked away
watching my world
shatter

watching me
nearly drown
you're back
because that
lonely
empty
shell
is full now

those teardrops
weren't a waste
of time
they rebuilt me
but you were
too impatient
to wait for the
construction
to be completed

your only
concern
was the
finished
product.

favorite hellos:

greet 2019 with a kind hug
and realistic expectations
she is young
inexperienced
trying her best to give
you all of the blessings
you ask for
in your midnight prayers

let her know that most mistakes are forgivable

guide her carefully
and reassure her from time to time

she is a gift made especially for you.

<u>hardest goodbyes:</u>

2018,
from me
you will receive
a farewell kiss
not a careless goodbye.

i grew up exposed to
sincere hugs,
goodbye kisses,
and never going to bed angry.
i grew up appreciating the value of a
real relationship.
i grew up seeing marriage as a gift and
not a trap.
i am lucky,
i am thankful,
i am one of the few,

thank you forever,
        mom and dad.

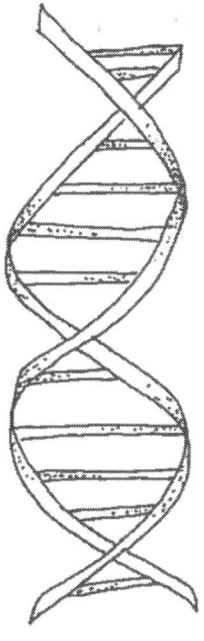

what has humanity come to
the old
the new
the adults
the children
each one discouraging the other
the intoxicating trait of
assuming your generation is
superior to the next
has been passed down
gene
to
gene
until those generations refuse to
accept the natural changes
the *progress*
that weaves through time
as the years turn

-we learn from the people who raised us

to the ones who have shaped me the most

family is two tall bud lights
and a black cherry soda
at pat's every Friday night
spending the evening amongst simple laughter
family is pancakes
and scalding hot bacon
cooked ten minutes before work on a Saturday
ready to go after sleeping in too late
family is a flour covered counter
the worn pages of a
great great....grandmother's cookbook
laying next to remnants of blueberry pie
family is a ten foot tall Christmas tree
cut down with a large dose of "fucks"
big, beautiful, *colored* lights strung around it
after arguing about white lights 15 minutes
before
family is a beat up couch in front of the fireplace
where everyone sits no matter how much room
there isn't
family is lunch and laundry on Sundays
talking around the kitchen table
making sure everyone is ready for Monday

family is 1 + 1 = 3

3 unique replicas of
2 amazing parents with
1 beautiful marriage

everything you do
everything you touch
everything you create
with your
bare
calloused
working
beautiful
hands
heart
mind
and
soul
you do in silence
sometimes
without appreciation
but
what amazes me
the most
is that you do it anyway
without a thought
for yourself.

-mothers

on the streets of London

the rain seemed to engulf
any warmth that attempted
to radiate from the street lamps
the umbrella you held
above our heads created
a sanctuary
from the madness around us
and even as Big Ben struck
midnight
i didn't feel as if we were
running out of time
the raindrops around us
had created a time machine
not one that moved *through* time
but one that simply
held the moment in place
refusing to let the endless motion
of the world disrupt it

things colored gray that seem to get forgotten:

the sky
right before the stars open their eyes
the time right after dusk when silence
seems to settle along the river bend
we used to walk beside
the pavement
along a winding path leading to that
tiny bookstore on the corner
where you offered to buy me anything
and i asked for a book of love poems
to remember you by
the sea
during the times when no one wants to visit
when Wind is whispering menacingly amongst
the waves and
Thunder is arguing carelessly with Lightening
neither of them ever stopping to look upon
the chaos they'd created
my eyes
standing in Terminal B the day you left
clutching a piece of graph paper that
felt less like a letter and more like a lifeline
i held onto as i allowed myself too many days of
tears before finally locking
those broken pieces
of my heart away for good.

i was born on a November morning
underneath a sunrise
the color of satin lilac

you were born on a summer evening
underneath a July moon
iron gray surrounding the stars
you took your first breath beneath

and although our first moments
in time itself
transpired under two very different skies
i truly believe that the stars aligned one day
and the autumn sun whispered gently
to the summer moon

Fate will paint a masterpiece with these two

maybe that's why the lavender in my eyes
mixes so well with the mood gray in yours

the two of us
woven together
underneath white linen sheets
creates the most beautiful work of art,
a tapestry even
Fate
would fail to weave.

and in the simplicity
of pen and paper
she created artwork
with her palette of black ink
on canvases of blue lines
she painted portraits
                landscapes
                abstract art
that even the most
accomplished illustrator
would struggle to recreate

-the power of words

whenever i am lost
in
my
mind
or
in
my
thoughts
the guidance i seek
is found when i
open
my
journal
and
uncap
my
pen

-writing is my compass

imagine the still silence
of an evening
at Cafe de Floré
the midsummer's moon
caressing the entire courtyard
in lunar magnificence
imagine soft lips
painted Paris red
with a rouge
even Marilyn Monroe
would approve of
imagine soft gray
moonlight
and
the silhouette
of a first kiss

-imagine the beginning of *us*

i remember it
perfectly
the pale pink dress
i was wearing
the warmth of the sun
on my face
as i looked up
and
kissed you
i remember the cafes
we passed
the ones with those
chocolate croissants
you liked so much

the memory
of our days in Paris
will remain in my mind
forever
iconic to me
as
the Eiffel Tower
is
to France

daily reminder 7:

fall in love with the most unpredictable version
of yourself.

let's be beautiful people
drinking good coffee
&
laughing with our heads
in the clouds

i think my fatal flaw
is holding onto
those

     what ifs
     daydreams
     those chimerical ideas
     that everyone around me
     keeps screaming are impossible

and
i couldn't be more
thankful
for that flaw

     i would rather die
     a thousand times
     in the midst
     of trying to make
     a dream
     into
     a reality
     then waste my
     beautiful
     irreplaceable chances
     on the silly cycle
     of *conformity*.

"don't feel as if you're at the end of your rope"

the wise words
my father spoke to me
when i was certain i no longer
had the strength to keep myself from
                    letting go
the wise words
that whispered encouragement
to the aching chambers of my heart
and reminded me that i had so many more
reasons to hold on
than i did to let go.

i've been trying to tell you to
fuck off
but the words always end up sounding like
i love you

-language barrier

the end of an evening cigarette

there were never

                any songs

that reminded me

                of you

that's how i knew

           you weren't the one

the sweetest words
that ever left your lips
were whispered
under the golden hues
of a Saturday afternoon's sun
you laid your hand
against the bare skin of my back
and pulled me closer
those soft words spilled
into the shimmering air
surrounding us
and fell gently
onto the white sheets
we were laying on

"you are absolute magic"

you said
with wonder in your eyes

"i could live a thousand lives

    and still fail to meet someone

      as utterly ethereal as you."

i tasted the stars
on my tongue
the moment my eyes closed
and
your lips pressed against mine.
that night,
our bodies were
another constellation
in the galaxy of lovers
just like us
before us,
but our insignificance
didn't even register in
either of our minds.

we were already lost
in an extraterrestrial world
of our own.

emelia grant

place your marble hands on my hips
let the gods carve us into one beautiful
masterpiece.
let them place our statue in museums.
let them wonder how we got so lucky
as to spend eternity in our own
unbreakable stone solace.

expectations

i refuse to settle for anything less
than a fairytale type of love
because
within the hopeless romanticism
of my antique heart
i've convinced myself
that there is another
timeless soul
who believes in magic
just as fiercely
as i do

i woke up to the soft brush of your finger against my cheek as you wiped away an errant tear, something i was used to, but it puzzled you so.

and when our eyes met you said to me

love,
there is
nothing
i want more
than to remove
every ounce
of heartache
i see in your eyes
when you're positive
i'm not looking.

it's a nearly impossible plight—
trying to express your feelings
when someone is constantly relating them
to *their* lives
instead of helping you understand them in order
to better *your* life.

the end of an evening cigarette

i wish we lived in a world
where spreading
real
love
was as easy as clicking
a tiny red heart
on the bottom left corner
of a picture

i can feel bitterness wrapping a cold, unforgiving hand around my nearly motionless heart. in the back of my mind, i know i should be fighting her, refusing to let her steal that last ounce of humanity from my weary heart. but the acceptance she offers, it's intoxicating. she paints a picture so beautiful, so *enticing*, that i'm practically begging her to strangle the last few heartbeats of hope i have left.

i am trying my best to the appreciate the small things: the dandelions and daisies, the rainy days, and the simplicity of sunshine falling on a freckled cheek. i am trying my best to become absolutely *enraptured* with the smell of an old book and the excitement that comes from opening a new one. i am trying my best to live a mindful life, and it is the most rewarding endeavor i have ever tried to achieve.

i think Fate
misplaced her golden thread
with the stem of a rose
when she started
weaving my
future
because
as soon as Love greeted me
in the form of a soft kiss & a crimson rose
i felt those bittersweet thorns
tearing their way through
the chambers of my
aching heart

there is an infinite difference
between loving someone,
being in love with the idea of someone,
and actually being *in love* someone.

be thankful

that you still see shapes
in the clouds

be thankful

that you still daydream
about magic and fairytales

be thankful

that you still consider a daisy to be
"he loves me, he loves me not"
instead of just a simple flower

be thankful

that you still have the imagination of a child

because that kind of creativity is rare
and
should be
cultivated
not
suppressed
under the pretense
of
growing up

we are so obsessed
with achieving the obvious
that appreciating the abstract
has become a foreign idea.

how toxic it is
to be raised in a society
where having opinions outside
of the cultural norm
is resented
for the risk it represents
instead
of praised
for the individuality it exudes.

-we must learn to live harmony

we are blessed with these beautiful
powerful
inspiring
capable
individual
voices
and yet we use them to argue
insult
attack
accuse
inflict *harm*
on each other
instead of weaving a melody
full of the complex harmonies possible
if only we took a moment
to respect one another
instead of tearing each other apart
at the first sign
of weakness.

if i could ask god for anything
i would ask him
to make me completely and utterly
fearless
because in my mind
there is no greater tragedy
than leaving the unknown of a possibility behind
in favor for the safety of a *what if*

be proud of yourself
be proud of your accomplishments
don't be ashamed
because the person next to you
might be smarter
or faster
or prettier

they're not you

the only life you are given to live
is your own
and that is a *privilege*
be proud of that privilege.

emelia grant

these blank pages
no longer offer me
any comfort.
i have written all of my
favorite hellos
and
said all of my
hardest goodbyes
i have broken
i have healed
i have come to a place
where the ink of my pen is empty
where *i* am empty.
what i need now
is time.

-goodbye for now

emelia grant

thank you:

miss rublee: for your eloquent style of teaching and inspiring; for showing me that art and writing go hand in hand together, taking the form of poetry; and for convincing me to take a leap of faith, and publish my artwork.

aida: for your kindness and honesty; for the many hours you spent reading, and editing, and inspiring me with your own exquisite artwork; and for the privilege of writing and publishing alongside you. it truly is an honor.

my beautiful family: (especially my parents) for your patience; for your encouragement; and for teaching me that, even though there is so much to cry about, laughter will always be the best medicine.

thank you for everything.

each and every one of you will always have a special place in my heart.

emelia grant

Growing up with her head in the clouds and her nose in a book, Emelia Grant followed her love of reading and found her true passion: writing. Based in Maine, her words—her artwork—are extensions of her own thoughts and experiences, and she hopes to provide a voice for the experiences of others. She spends a lot of her time at the town's local cafe, reading, writing, and listening to music. She plans on attending University of Maine Orono in the fall, where she is excited to learn even more about literature and writing. For more of her poetry, you can find her on Instagram @letters_to_the_lost.

Made in the USA
Middletown, DE
16 June 2019